CELLO

101 JAZZ SONGS

Available for
FLUTE, CLARINET, ALTO SAX, TENOR SAX, TRUMPET,
HORN, TROMBONE, VIOLIN, VIOLA, CELLO

ISBN 978-1-4950-2346-0

HAL•LEONARD®
CORPORATION
7777 W. BLUEMOUND RD. P.O. BOX 13819 MILWAUKEE, WI 53213

Visit Hal Leonard Online at
www.halleonard.com

CONTENTS

ALL OF ME

CELLO

Words and Music by SEYMOUR SIMONS
and GERALD MARKS

All the Things You Are

CELLO

Lyrics by OSCAR HAMMERSTEIN II
Music by JEROME KERN

APRIL IN PARIS

CELLO

Words by E.Y. "YIP" HARBURG
Music by VERNON DUKE

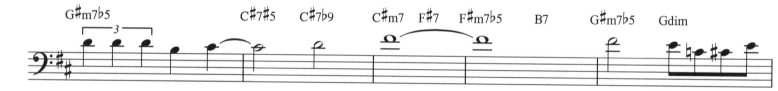

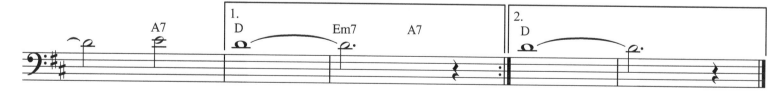

AUTUMN IN NEW YORK

CELLO

Words and Music by
VERNON DUKE

AUTUMN LEAVES

CELLO

English Lyric by JOHNNY MERCER
French Lyric by JACQUES PREVERT
Music by JOSEPH KOSMA

BEWITCHED

CELLO

Words by LORENZ HART
Music by RICHARD RODGERS

BEYOND THE SEA

Lyrics by JACK LAWRENCE
Music by CHARLES TRENET and ALBERT LASRY
Original French Lyric to "La Mer" by CHARLES TRENET

CELLO

THE BLUE ROOM

CELLO

Words by LORENZ HART
Music by RICHARD RODGERS

Moderately

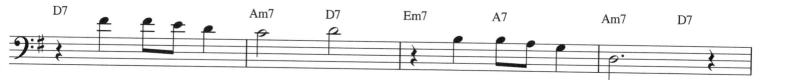

BLUE SKIES

Words and Music by
IRVING BERLIN

CELLO

BLUESETTE

Words by NORMAN GIMBEL
Music by JEAN THIELEMANS

BODY AND SOUL

Words by EDWARD HEYMAN,
ROBERT SOUR and FRANK EYTON
Music by JOHN GREEN

CELLO

BUT BEAUTIFUL

Words by JOHNNY BURKE
Music by JIMMY VAN HEUSEN

CELLO

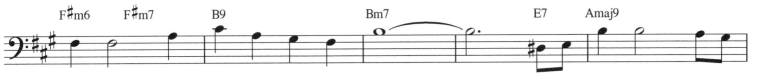

CAN'T HELP LOVIN' DAT MAN

Lyrics by OSCAR HAMMERSTEIN II
Music by JEROME KERN

CELLO

CARAVAN

CELLO

Words and Music by DUKE ELLINGTON,
IRVING MILLS and JUAN TIZOL

CHARADE

By HENRY MANCINI

CELLO

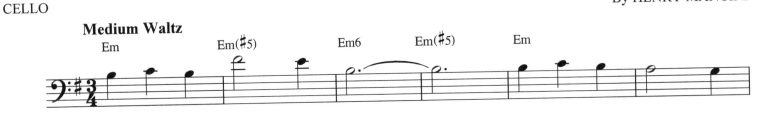

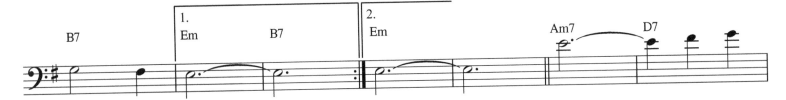

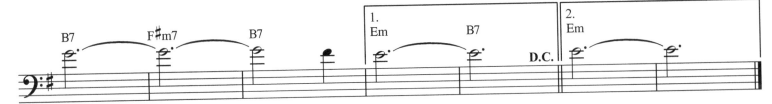

CHEEK TO CHEEK

CELLO

Words and Music by
IRVING BERLIN

COME RAIN OR COME SHINE

CELLO

Words by JOHNNY MERCER
Music by HAROLD ARLEN

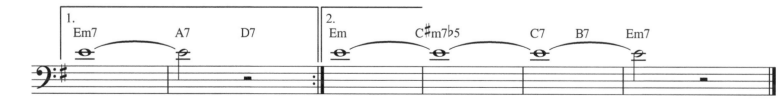

DANCING ON THE CEILING

CELLO

Words by LORENZ HART
Music by RICHARD RODGERS

DEARLY BELOVED

CELLO

Music by JEROME KERN
Words by JOHNNY MERCER

DO NOTHIN' TILL YOU HEAR FROM ME

CELLO

Words and Music by DUKE ELLINGTON
and BOB RUSSELL

DON'T GET AROUND MUCH ANYMORE

CELLO

Words and Music by DUKE ELLINGTON
and BOB RUSSELL

DREAMSVILLE

By HENRY MANCINI

CELLO

FALLING IN LOVE WITH LOVE

CELLO

Words by LORENZ HART
Music by RICHARD RODGERS

A FINE ROMANCE

Words by DOROTHY FIELDS
Music by JEROME KERN

FLY ME TO THE MOON
(In Other Words)

CELLO

Words and Music by
BART HOWARD

GEORGIA ON MY MIND

Words by STUART GORRELL
Music by HOAGY CARMICHAEL

CELLO

HERE'S THAT RAINY DAY

CELLO

Words by JOHNNY BURKE
Music by JIMMY VAN HEUSEN

HERE'S TO LIFE

CELLO

Music by ARTIE BUTLER
Lyrics by PHYLLIS MOLINARY

HONEYSUCKLE ROSE

CELLO

Words by ANDY RAZAF
Music by THOMAS "FATS" WALLER

Moderately, with a lilt

HOW DEEP IS THE OCEAN
(How High Is the Sky)

CELLO

Words and Music by
IRVING BERLIN

Slowly

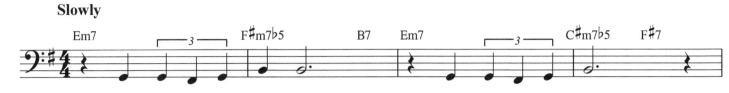

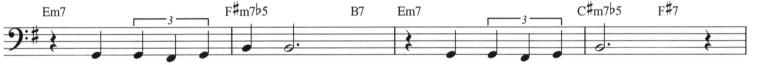

HOW INSENSITIVE
(Insensatez)

CELLO

Music by ANTONIO CARLOS JOBIM
Original Words by VINICIUS DE MORAES
English Words by NORMAN GIMBEL

Medium Bossa Nova

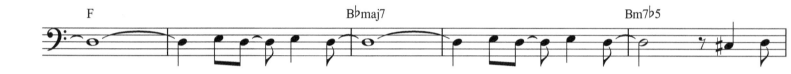

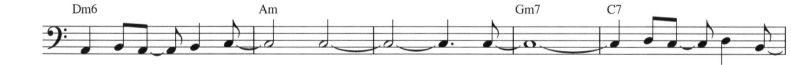

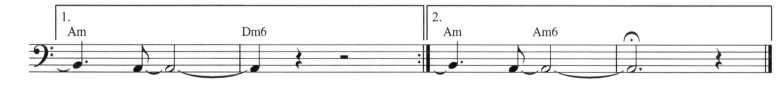

I CAN'T GET STARTED

CELLO

Words by IRA GERSHWIN
Music by VERNON DUKE

I COULD WRITE A BOOK

Words by LORENZ HART
Music by RICHARD RODGERS

CELLO

I GOT IT BAD AND THAT AIN'T GOOD

Words by PAUL FRANCIS WEBSTER
Music by DUKE ELLINGTON

Cello

I'LL REMEMBER APRIL

CELLO

Words and Music by PAT JOHNSTON,
DON RAYE AND GENE DE PAUL

I'M BEGINNING TO SEE THE LIGHT

CELLO

Words and Music by DON GEORGE, JOHNNY HODGES,
DUKE ELLINGTON and HARRY JAMES

Medium Bounce

I'VE GOT THE WORLD ON A STRING

CELLO

Words by TED KOEHLER
Music by HAROLD ARLEN

IF I WERE A BELL

CELLO

By FRANK LOESSER

IMAGINATION

Words by JOHNNY BURKE
Music by JIMMY VAN HEUSEN

CELLO

Slowly, with a lilt

IN A SENTIMEMTAL MOOD

By DUKE ELLINGTON

CELLO

IN THE WEE SMALL HOURS OF THE MORNING

CELLO

Words by BOB HILLIARD
Music by DAVID MANN

INDIANA
(Back Home Again in Indiana)

Words by BALLARD MacDONALD
Music by JAMES F. HANLEY

CELLO

ISN'T IT ROMANTIC?

CELLO

Words by LORENZ HART
Music by RICHARD RODGERS

IT COULD HAPPEN TO YOU

Words by JOHNNY BURKE
Music by JAMES VAN HEUSEN

CELLO

Moderately

IT DON'T MEAN A THING
(If It Ain't Got That Swing)

Cello

Words and Music by DUKE ELLINGTON
and IRVING MILLS

IT MIGHT AS WELL BE SPRING

Lyrics by OSCAR HAMMERSTEIN II
Music by RICHARD RODGERS

CELLO

THE LADY IS A TRAMP

Words by LORENZ HART
Music by RICHARD RODGERS

CELLO

LAZY RIVER

Words and Music by HOAGY CARMICHAEL
and SIDNEY ARODIN

CELLO

LET THERE BE LOVE

CELLO

Lyric by IAN GRANT
Music by LIONEL RAND

LIKE SOMEONE IN LOVE

CELLO

Words by JOHNNY BURKE
Music by JIMMY VAN HEUSEN

LITTLE GIRL BLUE

CELLO

Words by LORENZ HART
Music by RICHARD RODGERS

LONG AGO (AND FAR AWAY)

Words by IRA GERSHWIN
Music by JEROME KERN

'Cello

LOVER, COME BACK TO ME

CELLO

Lyrics by OSCAR HAMMERSTEIN
Music by SIGMUND ROMBERG

Moderately

LULLABY OF BIRDLAND

Words by GEORGE DAVID WEISS
Music by GEORGE SHEARING

CELLO

LULLABY OF THE LEAVES

CELLO

Words by JOE YOUNG
Music by BERNICE PETKERE

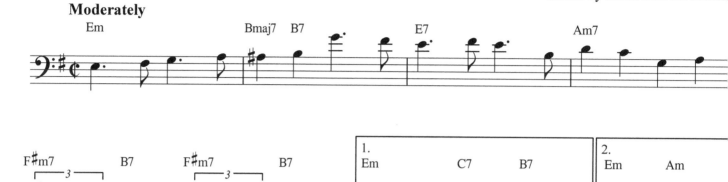

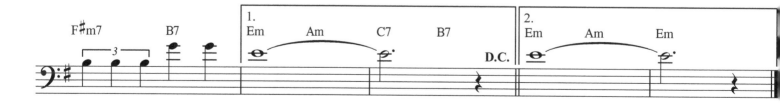

MANHATTAN

Words by LORENZ HART
Music by RICHARD RODGERS

ELLO

Medium Swing

MEDITATION
(Meditação)

Cello

Music by ANTONIO CARLOS JOBIM
Original Words by NEWTON MENDONÇA
English Words by NORMAN GIMBEL

Medium Bossa Nova

MIDNIGHT SUN

Words and Music by LIONEL HAMPTON,
SONNY BURKE and JOHNNY MERCER

MISTY

CELLO

Music by ERROLL GARNER

MOOD INDIGO

Words and Music by DUKE ELLINGTON,
IRVING MILLS and ALBANY BIGARD

CELLO

Moderately slow

MOONLIGHT IN VERMONT

Words by JOHN BLACKBURN
Music by KARL SUESSDORF

CELLO

MORE THAN YOU KNOW

Cello

Words by WILLIAM ROSE and EDWARD ELISCU
Music by VINCENT YOUMANS

MY HEART STOOD STILL

CELLO

Words by LORENZ HART
Music by RICHARD RODGERS

MY OLD FLAME

Words and Music by ARTHUR JOHNSTON
and SAM COSLOW

Cello

MY ONE AND ONLY LOVE

CELLO

Words by ROBERT MELLIN
Music by GUY WOOD

MY ROMANCE

Words by LORENZ HART
Music by RICHARD RODGERS

ELLO

MY SHIP

Words by IRA GERSHWIN
Music by KURT WEILL

CELLO

THE NEARNESS OF YOU

Words by NED WASHINGTON
Music by HOAGY CARMICHAEL

A NIGHT IN TUNISIA

CELLO

By JOHN "DIZZY" GILLESPI
and FRANK PAPARELL

Moderately fast Swing

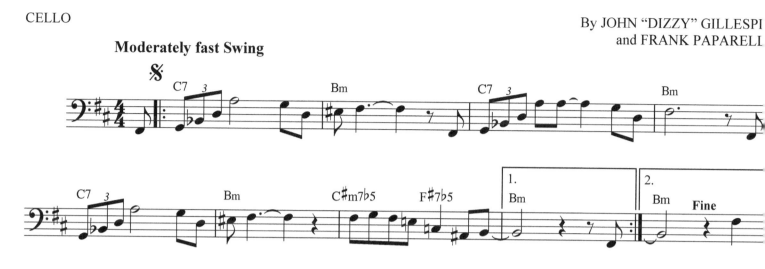

ON GREEN DOLPHIN STREET

Lyrics by NED WASHINGTON
Music by BRONISLAU KAPER

ONE NOTE SAMBA
(Samba de uma nota so)

CELLO

Original Lyrics by NEWTON MENDONÇA
English Lyrics by ANTONIO CARLOS JOBIM
Music by ANTONIO CARLOS JOBIM

Medium Bossa Nova

PICK YOURSELF UP

Words by DOROTHY FIELDS
Music by JEROME KERN

Cello

Moderately fast Swing

POLKA DOTS AND MOONBEAMS

Cello

Words by JOHNNY BURKE
Music by JIMMY VAN HEUSEN

QUIET NIGHTS OF QUIET STARS
(Corcovado)

CELLO

English Words by GENE LEES
Original Words and Music by ANTONIO CARLOS JOBIM

Medium Bossa Nova

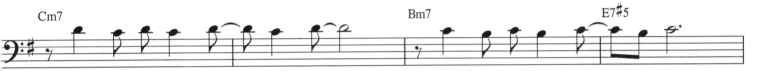

SATIN DOLL

CELLO

By DUKE ELLINGTON

SKYLARK

Words by JOHNNY MERCER
Music by HOAGY CARMICHAEL

CELLO

Moderate Swing

SO NICE
(Summer Samba)

CELLO

Original Words and Music by MARCOS VALLE
and PAULO SERGIO VALLE
English Words by NORMAN GIMBEL

Medium Bossa Nova

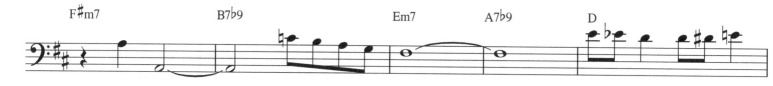

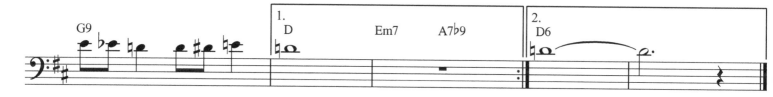

SOPHISTICATED LADY

CELLO

Words and Music by DUKE ELLINGTON,
IRVING MILLS and MITCHELL PARISH

SPEAK LOW

CELLO

Words by OGDEN NASH
Music by KURT WEILL

STELLA BY STARLIGHT

Words by NED WASHINGTON
Music by VICTOR YOUNG

Cello

STOMPIN' AT THE SAVOY

Cello

By BENNY GOODMAN
EDGAR SAMPSON and CHICK WEBB

Bright Swing

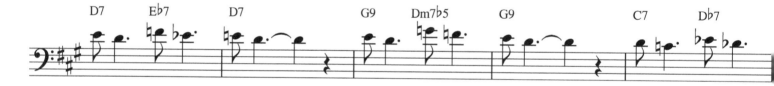

STORMY WEATHER
(Keeps Rainin' All the Time)

Lyric by TED KOEHLER
Music by HAROLD ARLEN

Cello

A SUNDAY KIND OF LOVE

Cello

Words and Music by LOUIS PRIMA, ANITA NYE LEONARD,
STANLEY RHODES and BARBARA BELLE

Moderate Swing

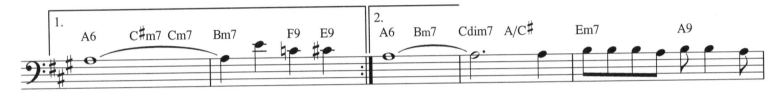

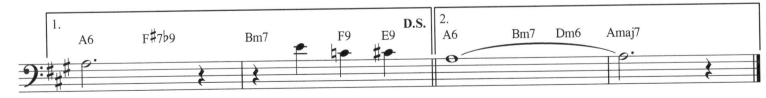

TANGERINE

Words by JOHNNY MERCER
Music by VICTOR SCHERTZINGER

ELLO

THERE'S A SMALL HOTEL

CELLO

Words by LORENZ HAR
Music by RICHARD RODGER

THESE FOOLISH THINGS (REMIND ME OF YOU)

ELLO

Words by HOLT MARVELL
Music by JACK STRACHEY

THE THINGS WE DID LAST SUMMER

CELLO

Words by SAMMY CAHN
Music by JULE STYNE

Moderate Swing

THIS CAN'T BE LOVE

Ello

Words by LORENZ HART
Music by RICHARD RODGERS

THOU SWELL

CELLO

Words by LORENZ HART
Music by RICHARD RODGERS

Moderately

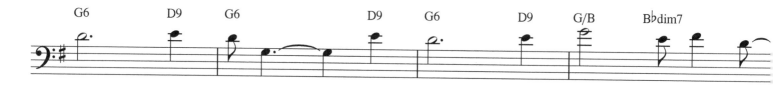

UNFORGETTABLE

Words and Music by
IRVING GORDON

CELLO

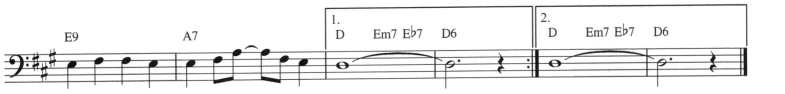

THE VERY THOUGHT OF YOU

Cello

Words and Music by
RAY NOBLE

With a slow, easy Swing

WATCH WHAT HAPPENS

Music by MICHEL LEGRAND
Original French Text by JACQUES DEMY
English Lyrics by NORMAN GIMBEL

CELLO

WAVE

CELLO

Words and Music b
ANTONIO CARLOS JOBIM

THE WAY YOU LOOK TONIGHT

Words by DOROTHY FIELDS
Music by JEROME KERN

CELLO

WHAT'LL I DO

CELLO

Words and Music by
IRVING BERLIN

WILLOW WEEP FOR ME

CELLO

Words and Music by
ANN RONELL

Slowly, with a lilt

WITCHCRAFT

CELLO

Music by CY COLEMAN
Lyrics by CAROLYN LEIGH

Moderately

Yesterdays

CELLO

Words by OTTO HARBACH
Music by JEROME KERN

YOU ARE TOO BEAUTIFUL

CELLO

Words by LORENZ HART
Music by RICHARD RODGERS

YOU BROUGHT A NEW KIND OF LOVE TO ME

Words and Music by SAMMY FAIN,
IRVING KAHAL and PIERRE NORMAN

CELLO

Medium Swing

YOU DON'T KNOW WHAT LOVE IS

CELLO

Words and Music by DON RAYE
and GENE DePAUL